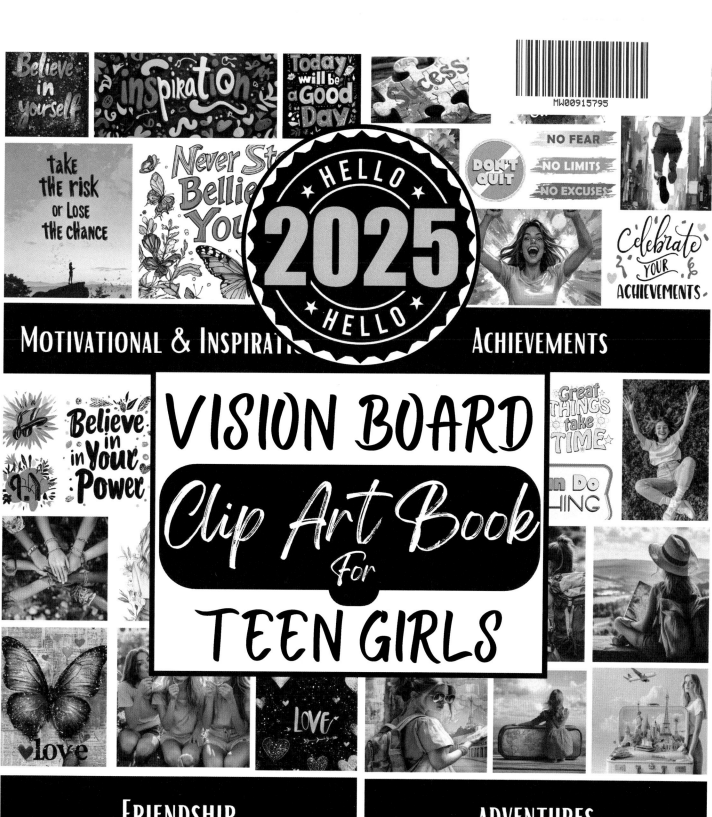

VISION BOARD
Clip Art Book
For
TEEN GIRLS

HELLO 2025 HELLO

MOTIVATIONAL & INSPIRATIONAL · ACHIEVEMENTS

FRIENDSHIP · ADVENTURES

ADVENTURES

Say Yes to new Adventures

time to travel

travel more

HOBBIES

Believe & Succeed

Success Follows Those Who Believe

DON'T QUIT

NO FEAR

NO LIMITS

NO EXCUSES

Celebrate YOUR ACHIEVEMENTS

Achievements

PROVE THEM WRONG, every, TIME

Great THINGS take TIME

You Can Do ANYTHING

SPIRITUALITY

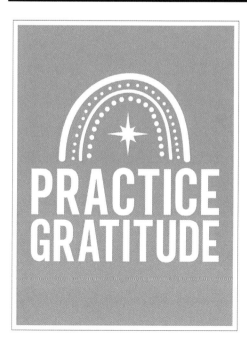

PRACTICE GRATITUDE

WHEN THINGS CHANGE INSIDE YOU, THINGS CHANGE AROUND YOU

Trust in The Universe

FRIENDSHIP

Fashion

HOME

FAMILY

Self-care.

SELFCARE

FINANCE

HEALTHY EATING

I DESERVE TO LIVE A LONG, HEALTHY LIFE

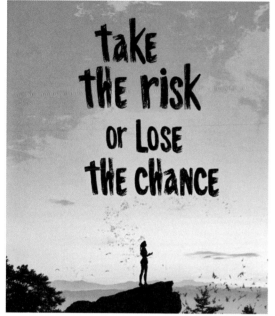

MOTIVATIONAL & INSPIRATIONAL

POSITIVE VIBES

BONUS IMAGES

Thank you!

We are thrilled to extend our heartfelt gratitude for your recent purchase of our **Vision Board Clip Art Book for Teen Girls**. Your support means the world to us, and we can't wait for you to explore the creative possibilities that await within its pages.

We believe that creating a vision board is an incredible journey towards manifesting your dreams and goals. With this clip art book, we aimed to provide you with a toolkit to make that journey even more exciting and visually engaging. We trust that the vibrant illustrations and versatile elements will empower your vision board to truly reflect your aspirations.

As you dive into your creative projects, we kindly request your feedback. Your thoughts are invaluable to us and to others who are considering enhancing their creative process with our book. If you have a moment to spare, we would greatly appreciate it if you could share your experience and insights in a few words on Amazon. Your honest review will help fellow dreamers make informed decisions and discover the magic of our **Vision Board Clip Art Book for Teen Girls**.

And one more thing I'd like to say...if you find the books **"2025 Vision Board Clip Art Book for Women"** and **"Positive Affirmations Vision Board Clip Art Book"** useful, you can find them on Amazon under the same author name, *Jasmine Eason.*

Wishing you endless inspiration and success as you craft your vision board masterpiece in 2025!

Warm regards,
Jasmine Eason

Made in the USA
Monee, IL
23 December 2024

75273618R00021